„ Who plans, wins ... "

Holistic Enterprise
Leadership

Activity-based Costing
Use & Implementation

Impressum

Bibliographic information of the German National Library
[Deutsche Nationalbibliografie]
The German National Library lists this publication in the
German National Library; Detailed bibliographic data are
available online at: http://dnb.dnb.de.

978-3-7451-0343-4 (Paperback)
978-3-7451-0344-1 (Hardcover)
978-3-7451-0345-8 (e-Book)

Cover picture: Gerald Plattner
Proofreading: Shannon Aubert
Illustrations: Guenther Pichler

Business Insights by Haufe

An imprint of Haufe-Lexware GmbH & Co. KG, Freiburg

A book for
entrepreneurs & managing
directors, and those who want
to be them ...

For ease of reading, some of the terms are used in a
gender-specific formulation. Of course, they are
equally applicable to all genders.

Foreword

Dear readers,

I am glad that you have found the 1st volume of my book: „ **Who plans, wins ...** “

With this book, I will take you to the world of corporate governance and management. Read this book and see how you can gain more efficiency and security in making decisions for the future with the "Integrated Corporate Management & Resource Consumption Accounting Method". The advantage of the corporate governance and management philosophy is the dynamic in the organization that guides employees in a positive direction. I hope you enjoy reading this book. Do you have questions, requests or suggestions? -

I look forward to hearing from you.

Günther Pichler

Hidden inefficiencies

To start this chapter, I would like to give you a specific example from my consulting career. This example answers the question, "why *analytical planning* is so important."

The following happened to me few years ago during a budgeting meeting with a customer:

When analyzing the cost types for clients, we usually work according to the Pareto principle 80:20. This means that if we have 100 cost types, then 20 of these cost types account for 80% of the specific cost. For this customer, the cost type "water" was ranked in 18th place.

The company's controller had decided not to invest the "water" cost type, and showed that the past five budgets had a consistent sum of water expenses.

The real question was: "Not where, but <u>what</u> did the company need the water for?"

In the course of the analytical planning we found out that the water was used to cool the machines. After detailed investigations, we discovered that even at maximum load and operating power of the machines, only half of the cost type "water" was used.

Now the real search began – looking for the second half of the water consumption. We analyzed the company's water usage for cleaning, coffee, hand washing, showers in the changing rooms, etc.

The analysis of the second half of the water was ultimately not successful. Therefore, we decided to try something different, and read the water meter on Friday after work and then again on Monday morning. It turned out that the meter went on, although all machines were not in use. Has someone secretly tapped the water?

No, there was no water being diverted. The main line had a leak above the meter! So, the water dripped from the pipe and seeped into the grounds unused - for years!

The cost of water per cubic meter amounts to about 1, - € and the sewage fee is set at 2, - per cubic meter.

Therefore, the company tried to successfully negotiate with the waterworks or the wastewater organization, at least over the sewage charges.

My conclusion: This type of overhead planning has already enabled many customers to discover the types of costs which have cost them enormous sums of money year in, year out.

Are you sure that the electricity of the neighboring building is not connected to your electricity meter?

The basis of the Greko method

- Transparency in all areas

- Business overview

- Security in making decisions

- Independent teams

Figure 1 Water tap

The Greko method

Each entrepreneur and manager broods about poor business processes and unachieved goals for hours, every day.

The Greko method has evolved over years to master the increasing complexity in companies. For performance and cost data, it is **a tailor-made management concept adjusted to the corporate culture**. It lays the foundation for a clearly structured process which can easily be navigated. This creates free space for potential development of employees in all areas.

On the one hand, Greko is a method, on the other hand, the Greko Software supports this method as a tool for successful implementation.

Greko is based on the principles of the process compliant Resource Consumption Accounting as taught by Hans Georg Plaut. While the length of the name may be daunting, it is nothing to be afraid of. There is no black box or secret code, everything can be explained using common sense. Greko gives companies answers where other technologies do not know them and cannot further the understanding of its users.

People often say, "This technology works only in production-based companies." However, a credit agency bank has been using the Greko method successfully for more than 30 years.

Every employee in the company works on production - the results are just not individual work pieces, but rather nodes of "information", with all the processes and steps behind it, which are necessary to satisfy the customer's needs. Mastering the complexity means connecting, visualizing and accounting all processes that work for each other.

We call this process internal cost allocation. In the age of Industry 4.0 performance surveys are no longer a subject of discussion, which means there is nothing stopping an increase in benefits or inspiration for the employee

Your advantages:

- More time for the essentials (innovation, employees, customers, family, leisure, etc.)
- Tailored calculations
- Visualization of process costs
- Information for more decision-making security
- Enthusiastic employees
- Increased customer satisfaction
- Strengthened leadership acceptance
- Personal responsibility amongst employees

Why do we want to do this to us?

Maybe I should tell you how I got to Greko (the process compliant Resource Consumption Accounting):

As an executive in a family business, I was responsible for moving a warehouse from point A to point B.

Naturally, there were monthly meetings in order to do comparisons of the planned budget with the actual budget.

The planning assumptions accounted for 160 service hours per month. There were "negative" deviations in my department on a monthly basis. It was exceedingly frustrating for me, because this caused me to regularly take on more projects than I was able to complete during regular working hours. We always made sure the quality and deadlines of the projects were met, but this of course meant that my department just had to do much more work!

In reality the plan-actual-data comparison or actual billing was a collection of cost types on cost centers. This meant there was no performance allocation. Even though I had done more work than my colleagues, spending much greater hours on a monthly basis doing this work, and outperformed them with these setbacks, it actually made me worse off than them! It was then that I decided to look for a **fair** settlement system or to develop one if I did not find one that was adequate.

In the course of my education and further training, a few years later, as a commercial manager, I restructured a subsidiary. It was during my training that I came across "Greko".

From that time on, I had an instrument that connected the costs and performance which allowed them to be calculated as process costs all across the company.

And so, the marginal cost was accordingly adjusted to performance. Thus, we developed a "fair" performance report instrument that could be used to calculate the work provided by means of a cost rate, wherever the performance occurred.

That is when an important question arose:

"Not where did the costs come from, but for what performance?"

With this question communication increases enormously and brings executives and coworkers around a table. You need to have all the information on hand that explains the performance precisely, the costs and the allocations of cost centers, projects, orders and cost objects. Only then, with all of this detailed information, it is possible to improve the whole process.

We always find enormous "know how" within the companies. All you need to do is to involve the employee teams, processing management, and IT in the procedure within the organization and, of course, do the quality checks, which are prepared to analyze and improve processes.

However, without costs, you never know if you are right!

Each one of the employees can follow their performance - cost center, reference quantity, sub-process - where they are charged in the cost object calculation.

At the end of the day, we have all the information for:

- Corporate management
- Employees who cause the costs
- Pre- and post-costing
- Contribution accounting

Now, responsible teams see the costs in relation to their performance as a price tag! The effect is immense. Just think of the projects that have been calculated with price tags (cost rates) that run over a longer period of time.

At the heart of this job is the management of cost center costs and services. The monthly target with actual data comparison makes the deviations transparent and can be easily corrected. Thus, the calculated prices of our products and services are always in focus.

Can you imagine attending a meeting with all of this data being readily available to all? Target costing becomes obvious when you are trying to find out which processes are variable and how they affect the overall costing process of the products and services.

In the course of quantity and price planning, we have integrated simulations - meaning "What if - when functions" - at the push of a button on the capacity shortage of employees and/or machines!

Employees need security and a method that provides transparency and understandable information. Employees want to be guided, to be led to reach their targets. On the one hand, complexity must be overcome to facilitate this, but on the other hand, teams must still be able to communicate the complex innovative process improvements in the organization.

This creates momentum in the company, which is extremely important for the development of the employee teams.

Figure 2 Source: Organization Koechert – contribution margin

The beauty of the Greko philosophy is that, the employees show the results of their performance in an honest, fair manner, e.g. via intranet.

That brings about trust and the urge to improve (CIP a continuous improvement process). A side effect of improving is the performance innovation.

If you use a software tool like Greko, you also take on the leadership philosophy, which the tool is based on.

As managers, we have an obligation to guide our employees to models of development and process simulation. Employees need be guided in such a way that the implementation of a new system is seen as a positive, and even fun, giving them the desire to get involved in the this new framework.

The basic requirement for this is a clearly formulated and strategic goal. Details on this topic can be found in : "Strategy Development with System Integrated Corporate Management by Mercedes".

It is interesting to see that many companies do not use these proven management methods, but instead they want to try reinvent everything time and time again.

It seems as though they are extremely busy and, with all their efforts, they do not notice that money is being wasted, dripping from the company's pipes, without any significant improvement on the outcome.

It can be compared to a woodworker who has a blunt saw and says: "I do not have time to sharpen the saw, I have to cut down trees!" Being stuck in the thought process of: "we've always done it this way" must end for results to change.

The time when "only" the managers have done the thinking work is over. The solution means autonomous self-management of teams. Delegate responsibility to teams!

The organizational form of the pyramid must give way to the cell organization. Situational decisions mean that "everyone" is a part of the company's success and therefore bears responsibility!

The Greko method brings for the business management the following:

Advantages:

- Understanding of all business processes
- Focus on customers
- Clarity in decisions & implementation
- Responsible thinking & acting
- Flexibility in the applicability
- Reduction of endless meetings
- More time for the essentials

Figure 3 old Orga-Form vs. new (Niels Pfläging 2013 Wiesbaden)

„ Unproductive, but not lazy! "

Out of 60 minutes of working time, only 37 minutes are productive

Czipin Consulting study on productivity in Austria Source: media.net 2013

Out of 60 minutes only 37 are productive = 61.6% - that's the equivalent of 85 unproductive days a year!

Out of those, there is:

5% work ethic and long breaks

8% IT problems

6% too little training

5% bad communication

The reasons for those aspects are a bad organization and a "poor" management style!

"The reason for not using the potential is not necessarily the employees' fault, but rather the poor planning."

Czipin says the goal should be 51 minutes!

1. Clearly define work processes
2. Arrange achievable goals with the teams
3. Transfer of necessary responsibility

In the business processes, we see the specification of goals as a major challenge for employees in teams. Only employees who work on site and in the upstream and downstream processes are able to take over the planning and management.

„ It can work differently "

Dm-Drogieriemarkt, a drug store. Market researchers describe the most successful brand in German retailing as a "prime example of a sustainable and continuously improving service promise".

A great example of this is the dm-Drogeriemarkt (a drug store), found around on every corner, and a part of very day lives, functioning in the form of decentralized network organization and implementing this leadership approach.

In my hometown I know all dm employees personally. Each one of them has an outstanding education, giving them the confidence to handle and take on all of the work processes that occur in their stores. There is no one boss!

The shelves are always well stocked and tidy. If you do not know where to find a product or have a question, someone will always be there to help you, and with a smile.

The cash register re-orders all of their products automatically. With this system, it appears as if the atmosphere and relationship between employees if full of respect and team-work.

And you can see their success!

Current situation

The ratios of growth, profitability, security, and full employment are in disarray in many industries, markets, and companies.

For the ones who miss the connection, "the times are becoming worse", and the "competition is becoming tougher". For those who blame others for their own problems, it remains hidden that with every decision postponed they lose *time and thus money*. That means that you have to learn to become better than the competition and not to blame others for the "bad times".

What topics do you have?

- More demanding customers
- Clear communication
- Correct information
- Rising costs
- Lack of transparency
- Unmotivated employees

Every organization has individual demands on the product / market combination. Therefore, executives are required to provide their teams with the information as a service. To support that, a customer-oriented service catalog with transfer prices should be created.

The customer and the team are in focus. Everything else must be reconsidered! The transformation is nothing other than rethinking how to set up the organization in the future. Decentralized network organizations need customizing services such as: clear rules to adhere to, and better communicated and clear information to create transparency throughout the company for employees.

Each company has a maturity level in terms of business model, structural & process organization, business processes, product lifecycle, culture, and learning and knowledge transfer to create and implement innovation.

Of course, in most companies there is cost accounting - at least that is what the management believes. Usually it is a cost collection on rough cost centers; the remaining costs are simply split at the end.

Requirements

The dilemma starts with the startling fact that the real costs are often unknown. More transparency and greater efficiency are required. Believe me, if you had the real costs of your products and services, you would make different choices.

- Verification of the calculation, the customer benefit and the product / market combination
- Finding talents for implementation of the goals set within the company
- Concentrating on the company's core competencies
- Evaluating & using marketing opportunities
- _Measurably_ improving value chains
- Teams independent goals development and improvements

Strategy development with system

Before you start with the activity-based costing, please create a budget plan and a financial plan.

With financial planning, you get an important statement in regards to the vital lifeline - the *"liquidity"*.

For planning, you firstly need "the" inspiring strategy; one that can be communicated within the company. Employees must be proud of their company.

They have to BELIEVE that they are part of the BEST company. It is immensely important for employees to know how they can find ways to contribute to the total value of their company.

Where does the data for marketing come from? Without the analyses of sales figures, price quality, product & customer contribution margins, nothing really works!

Which activities generate revenue increases? Are the costs of the effort really considered and calculated?

Stagnation means regression!

Almost all cultures that did not evolve and change, ended up vanishing from existence. According to Albert Deyhle, there is a WAY [German: WEG] for success – if you don't go the WAY, you're going to be gone with time!

- Growth (Wachstum) –
- Development (Entwicklung) –
- Profit (Gewinn)

The name of our company is

advanced profit control.

By that, we mean steering the profit and driving development in order to reach the growth target.

Marketing needs detailed analyses of:

- CM by customers
- CM by products
- CM by sales channels
- CM by sellers

In the eyewear factory perspective Inc. targets are displayed transparently. From this, the planning premises and the visualization for sales and revenue planning are derived.

Three products and their development for the next year.

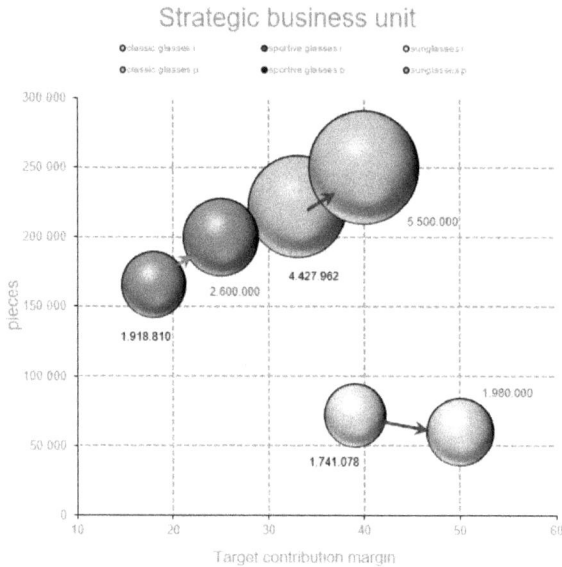

Figure 4 Source Pichler Target Turnover Planning

The most effective strategy development system is the system according to the method of Remmel. Imagine a hairline cross, divided into 4 Qs. It works counterclockwise.

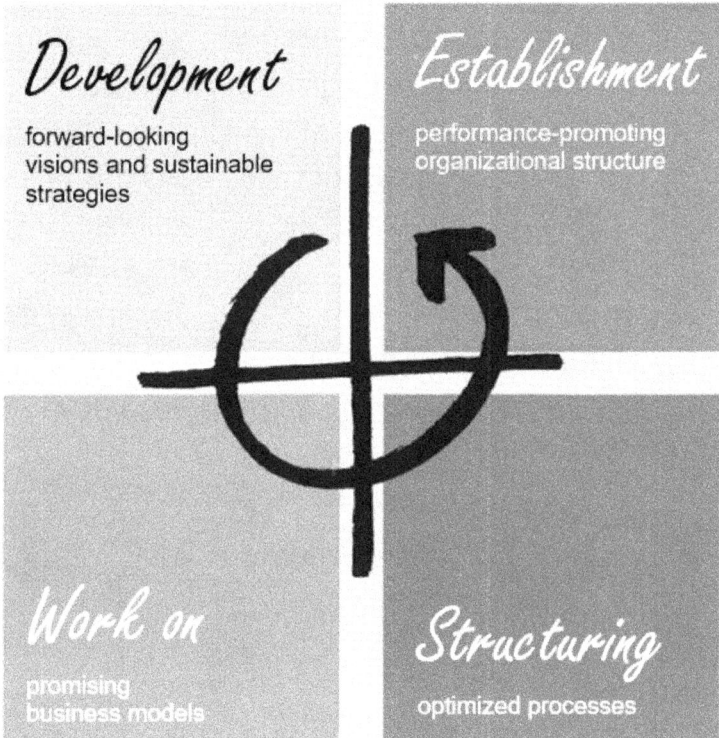

Figure 5 Source © Remmel 4 Q's

Strategy development

- Initiating or procuring market and competition analyses
- Evaluation of the product / market portfolio on existing / new markets & products
- Plausibility check of the strategic sales and earnings targets of the various product / market combinations
- Assessing alternative business models
- Analysis & evaluation of the depth of the added value (make or buy)
- Investigation of cooperation needs / opportunities

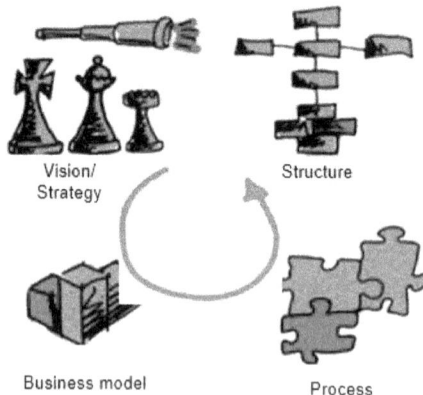

Figure 6 Source Remmel 4 Q's Model

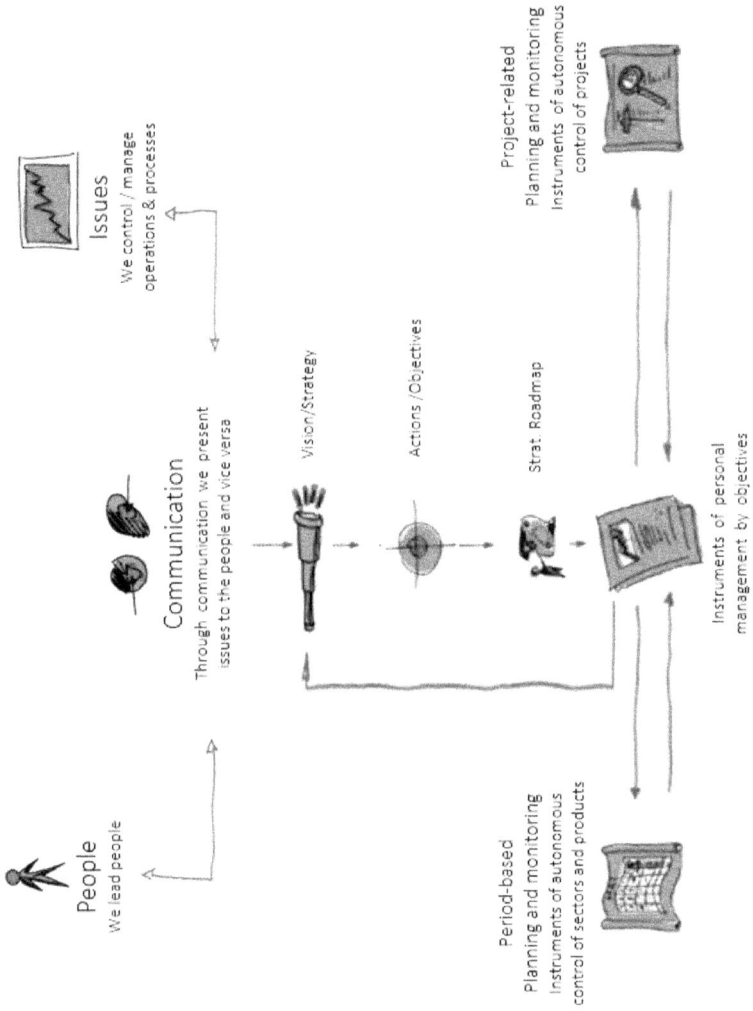

Figure 7 Source Remmel Philosophy of Leadership

Strategy implementation on the process & structural level

- Definition and analysis of business processes with the aim of minimizing interfaces

- Optimization of business processes, based on personalized measures and goals held in Balanced Scorecard - after clarification of possible target conflicts between the parties involved in the process, product-, area-, or project-related planning and monitoring

- To ensure that the introduction of a BSC is truly accepted by all, you must not only formulate hard-money targets such as sales, contribution margin, cost reduction, etc., but also understand how to develop soft goals, e.g.: "a concept is ready on ..." or: "in the innovation development, there is a finished prototype of ..."

- Employees and management teams set the quality criteria for management performance

Eyeware Factory Perspective [Glasses Unit]

Balanced Scorecard (BSC) Ebene 0

II. Customer / market perspective

S/O	Measures & goals	Events	Metrics	Own-Assessment	External-		
K18/1	Analysis of the existing A customer sports glasses, intensive customer care for "damage limitation"	end of December	Sales / DB Number of customers / potential		89%	25%	25%
						100%	
K18/2	Selective customer care outside the previous core markets	beginning of August	Sales / DB Number of customers / potential	89%	90%	95%	
K18/3	Forcierung des "Neuproduktes" Sonnenbrillen IV bei B Kunden in den Kernmärkten	end of June	Sales / DB Sunglasses IV		91%		
K18/4	"New customer acquisition sports glasses" "Ultra" in previous core markets "	early May	Sales / DB sports glasses "Ultra"	89%	90%	95%	
K18/5	Enhanced Customer Care Classic Glasses with existing customers in core markets "	Beginning of September	Sales / DB Number of customers / potential				

Figure 8 Source Remmel & Günther Pichler Scorecard

advanced profit control
apx consulting GmbH

53

How do you generate innovations?

We are developing a "d. o. n. i." meaning: day of new ideas. We expect and encourage employees to deliver new ideas - over and over again ...

Many strategy projects are neither properly set up nor pursued according to the plan and there is certainly no project controlling. Strategy development does not mean that the boss and a consultant lock themselves up in a room and produce some slides!

It needs much more, and above all, it requires team leaders, employees, customers, suppliers, creative thinkers, and after

Carl Gustav Jung - Insights Discovery®, that is where blue and green employees are needed, as well as the red and the yellow ones. It really is team work, involving everyone in the company, to get the most out of the unexplored opportunities.

This technology could be a base, and using it in different cases helps the organization create a conversation in which everyone is able to communicate and understand each other better.

It is important to deal with the error culture, you learn from mistakes and can then also try something new.

8 steps to the activity-based costing

The Greko activity-based costing is a resource consumption accounting theory that refers to indirect business units.

The costs are planned according to activities and charged to the process-cost calculation using the cost rate (price list for the activity). In most companies, there is clarity about the "productive" costs: material usage, external services, machine and employee hourly rates.

But what about the "unproductive" costs, such as administration, sales, IT, research and development? How should these costs be offset against the product and service calculation? In most companies, it happens in the form of more or less dubious overhead surcharges.

Do not be afraid of the performance, I have already experienced my miracles. This went from dismissal of the praise of employees who wanted to be measured or who would have expected feedback on their performance.

The goal of activity-based-costing is to improve planning, management, and control of indirect areas. We have to get away from ambiguous overheads, we owe it to the teams that have been working hard, and loyal to the company!

Step 1. Revenue planning
Sales and turnover planning

The objective should be: "increase sales, sell more, increase selling prices and reduce price deductions, such as discounts."

An essential part of our success is the challenge of innovation. The unique selling proposition (USP) only works if we really have one!

We collect data such, as sales per customer, or discounts and the contribution margins in our IT systems throughout the year.

Collecting and evaluating information from customers, suppliers and competitors is also important. Think about the people; who were the first ones have the contact with the customers, and were the last?

Simply call up your company yourself and experience how you are treated. How long does it take for the phone to be answered? What happens if you call again after working hours?

These links between customers and our company are vital. Do you have a clear communication concept for these functions? What if the customer asks questions? What can an end user point "mechanic, waiter, salesman or our truck driver" say about the delivery by our company? If there are complaints, how are they handled? Do you have a book of complaints that is accessible to all employees?

Just at this point, each of these employees has the opportunity to find out the buying habits and needs of the customers and to pass this information on to the company.

This way they recognize customer-specific, regionally limited, or seasonal optimization potential, as well as measures to improve sales and revenue generation.

The first evaluations of sales controlling are followed by the consideration of the relationships between the effort cost taken to find a new customer, inquiries for offers, and actual offers for orders. In order to do this, you need to collect the required data throughout the year. The analysis provides valuable information on how many orders arose from a certain number of inquiries and/or offers.

This way, it can be determined on a cross-sales basis where improvements can be made in the acquisition process and in the processing of requirements and inquiries in order to win more orders with a high contribution margin.

Cluster your customers and products with the ABC analysis into units that the sales team can control in a better way.

Do you also confront your sales staff with the topic of "working capital" and outstanding debts? Often, it is just a minor matter why a customer has not paid you.

Take the opportunity to talk with the customer - it pays off!

Key figures for sales optimization:

Analyzing market volume & saturation point

Supporting sales representatives as well as demanding from them

Analyzing product / market combination

Contribution margin and price quality

Discounts

Outstanding debts and complaints

Analyzing customer benefits according to Jochen Schauenburg

Customer satisfaction

Customer loyalty

Visit efficiency

In addition to classic sales planning, you should always carry out sales planning with quantities.

It lays the foundation for the subsequent planning of purchasing quantities, production quantities, capacities, and the capacities that you analyze for short supplies during the planning process.

Your advantages

- You increase sales volume and revenue through analysis and targeted focused planning and actual variances

- You create a binding target

- You set measures based on plan / actual comparisons

- You reduce revenue reductions (discounts, bonuses and reimbursements)

Step 2. Structure of the structural data

I highly recommend using an IT program for the introduction. Without an IT program, you will not be able to stay on track. In the eyewear factory Inc., they used the IT program Greko.at.

Structure of the data:

- Cost centers
- Cost types
- Cost objects
- Orders
- Human resources
- Activities
- Customers base
- Products base, etc.

Tailored controlling

The new challenges of transformation and digitalization, as well as the new business models that are necessary for the survival of the business, processes, and process costs are *always* in focus.

At every ICV Controller Congress in Munich, the big bosses of SAP, Siemens, Lufthansa etc. always talk about the importance of process management and process costs. Companies with new business sales models, but with the "autonomous self-management", are the ones that tend to draw the greatest amount of attention.

The magic words today are flexibility combined with fast simulation methods.

Design your control rationally. Manage to visualize the target, allowing you to gain valuable information, and thus make substantial important decisions in the direction of new business models.

Your employees will set higher and higher demands on controlling in the future. Only with a controlling system that is tailored to the needs of your organization will valuable employees stay, and new talent be attracted to work with you.

Step 3. Planning price tags
Determination of cost rates

The planning of cost centers starts with the above-mentioned structural data. These costs are then charged in the form of cost rates = price tags by means of performance volume to the recipients (cost objects).

If there is already a supposed cost accounting, which "only" represents a cost collection with allocations, you need to take this data as a basis for planning of the cost centers.

If no account assignment of the cost types to cost centers and cost units has been carried out in the financial accounting, then you will need to use the balance list to compile an operational analysis sheet (OAS).

A nice side effect of developing the OAS operational analysis sheet is that the responsible employees get to know the cost structure of the company and, of course, see their own department in a new light.

If you have the accounting journal lines accounted by cost centers available from the financial accounting, you should transfer them to the master planning of the cost center accounting. After that is done it is possible to create the cost center planning of the primary costs.

All media reports on the benefits of modern leadership and autonomous self-management, but this requires the necessary foundation for implementation in order to function properly.

The Greko method, after appropriate preparation, delivers the price tags, and provides the basis for each employee to transparently present their performance. The executives and employees have the opportunity to inspect their performance, to check the target achievements, and this allows them to set up the feedback system. Praise, recognition, and appreciation continue to motivate the employees.

The existing clearing systems create dubious overheads, which are distributed like a watering can and thus do not guarantee a meaningful calculation.

Determination of cost rates for meaningful calculations.

By actively offsetting the internal services processes one receives completely different cost rates, in terms of resource planning, it is very exciting for all cost center managers to plan these as a precautionary measure - so that all sender and receiver are responsible ...

planning sheets

cost center	120	Bookkeeping	✓ AU allocation	CT setting		1,200.0 #
Work	1	Eyeware Factory Ltd.		responsibility:	LEH Martin Lehner	Debit dunning

comment on

LU	CTY	description	VT	W	CC	AU	ORC	OU	Quantity	price	total	variances	%XR
3010	00001	# process planning						Std.	213.3	0.000	0	0	0
0110	62000	Salaries						Std.	277.2	17,333	4,806	4,806	4,806
0111	90550	Salaries Related Costs (SRC)					500500	%	4,806.6	0.610	2,931	2,931	2,931
0114	78000	Employee Training						EUR	0.2	2,103,751	473	473	473
0260	76000	office supplies						EUR	0.0	0.000	56	56	0
0270	77550	Legal and consulting fees						EUR	0.0	0.000	338	338	338
0280	73900	Postage and postal costs						EUR	0.0	0.000	51	51	51
0301	92001	AU Building costs	K	1	200	1		m²	1.1	18,982	21	21	21
0310	92101	AU Electricity costs	K	1	210	E		kWh	11.3	0.064	1	1	0
0320	92201	AU IT process costs	K	1	220	A		EStd	28.2	29,719	837	422	415
0330	92301	AU Communication	K	1	230	1		ERH	2,254.0	0.151	339	270	69
0900	90900	calc. depreciation						EUR	0.0	0.000	124	124	124
1999	99990	Secondary fixed costs	K	1	230	1		ERH	2,224.0	0.024	55	55	55
1999	99990	Secondary fixed costs	K	1	220	A		EStd	1.1	25.627	0	0	0
1999	99990	Secondary fixed costs	K	1	210	E		kWh	28.2	0.027	0	0	29
1999	99990	Secondary fixed costs	K	1	200	1		EStd	28.2	5.481	154	0	154
0100									0.0	0.000	0	0	0

	total	variances	%XR
planned costs	10.216	9.010	1.206
planned costs rates	8.513	7.508	1.005

Figure 9 Planning sheet Cost Centre

74

How does the activity-based costing work?

In the activity-based costing, main processes (cost centers) are broken down into sub-processes. And then, these sub-processes are broken down again into activities. The activities are assigned objectively across cost centers.

Example:

Main process: Accountancy

Sub-prices: Management of receivables

Activities: Credit check, new customers, invoicing, dunning, debt collection

In the next step, the activities are recorded in reference quantities, e.g. number of hours for maintenance of the customer base, number of bookings of outgoing invoices, number of checks on deductions, discounts, number of credit checks, number of reminders.

Knowing the recipient (of the service) is crucial information in activity-based costing. To whom have we provided the above-mentioned services for? Do not worry, ladies and gentlemen, the data for the performance recording is usually in all databases of your company. If you build a modern system in the sense of Industry 4.0, then there must be no "tally charts"!

The planning of activities is the prerequisite for specifications - as well as in production. And it is the basis for productivity measurement. Thus, each cost center manager gets a tool in their hand to lead their own area.

What does the abc bring?

The previously unallocated administrative cost centers or the structural costs (effort costs - fixed costs) are dissolved. Now, these cost centers can be accounted as "productive" cost centers for individual products and services.

The costs of the individual processes and the performance volume create transparency that everyone understands. The responsible teams recognize opportunities for rationalization and increased productivity.
The teams can autonomously organize all processes better *and* more efficiently.

Your advantages

- Each activity gets a price tag attached
- The teams develop standard time for activities themselves
- Cost awareness arises
- Unproductiveness and inefficiencies are recognized
- Transparency greatly improves decisions
- Productivity increases
- Deviations are detected quickly
- Monthly measurements make improvements easier
- Success rating of overhead cost centers
- Resources become available for innovation projects
- Transfer prices internal cost allocation - OECD compliant

Step 4. Internal cost allocation
Cost centers which provide for others

The activity-based internal cost allocation are costs of a cost center, which bill their performance x price tag (cost rate) to another cost center.

This allocation represents one of the most important cost information of a good activity-based costing to get the true cost of a cost center. Experience has shown that the cost share of a cost center often exceeds the 50% mark.

We assume that as far as possible all cost centers / performance, as well as the administrative and distribution cost centers, will be **"charged"** to cost objects, orders and projects.

This brings a new approach for employees to see themselves as autonomous team leaders with cost and performance figures.

Firstly, with this new technology, the elements of modern leadership emerge, the *target achievement*, as the highest level of motivation according to Herzberg - in the sense of working out, and on autonomous goals.

Secondly, it creates a fair, fact-based *feedback system,* or in other words, the *recognition and appreciation* that people need.

So far, no one has spoken with the financial accounting performance measures and because of this fact, it did not come to the above-mentioned feedback, and that is because the costs of the financial accounting were simply split with a key factor!

Of course, the financial accounting provides performance which is enormously important for the further processing information, but extra special care must be taken in the introduction of activity-based costing in all administrative areas.

One cost center is the "sender" and the other the "recipient". In the normal planning, the sender starts to plan the costs and performance and to charge x price tag to the recipient by means of performance volume.

In order to determine the required capacities from the sender, the latter announces their need for required performance of a cost center / reference quantity.

This creates a commercial contract between the sender and the recipient. Firstly, the price (performance price list) and secondly, the planned decrease in the performance.

Employees want to display their work performance and, more importantly, they want to be awarded for it. When was the last time you rewarded your employees in financial accounting, quality assurance, building services, etc.? Figure 10 shows the cost center financial accounting, which is usually set as an overhead rate in the administration.

As you can see, you make all unproductive cost centers billable now! (Performance of Bookkeeping)

1	120	Financial accounting	1	bookings	book	30.000.0
1	120	Financial accounting	2	Debtors bookings	invi	6.000.0
1	120	Financial accounting	3	Debit customer base	Num	2.000.0
1	120	Financial accounting	4	Debit credit check	Num	250.0
1	120	Financial accounting	5	Debit dunning	warn	1.200.0
1	120	Financial accounting	6	Edit debit outages	Aski	20.0
1	120	Financial accounting	7	Debit letters write	Mail	210.0

Each employee provides performance that contributes to the overall success. We no longer distinguish between productive and unproductive cost centers!

And only in this way, the basis for the "autonomous self-management" arises.

What do you think, how do employees feel when the performance is transparent and is presented to colleagues for the first time?

Many employees work voluntarily, without salary, at associations, or are even world champions in triathlons because they do not feel promoted and needed at work. They will find a different way to spend their time, and a different place to excel, displaying their skills.

Employees know their performance potential!

Step 5. Structure of the calculations
Cost objects - calculation

In order to make the calculation transparent, we recommend the application of an accounting contribution.

This way, all employees see their performance in the calculation and it creates a communication between the employees and their processers.

Only if you measure process steps in such a way and present it accordingly, you can sustainably improve them.

The structure of cost units always depends on the width and depth of the assortment. How detailed should you go at the beginning, depends on the available data and the data preparation.

In some cases, you have already achieved a great amount by creating a first calculation on product groups.

This time, the sender is the cost center and the recipient is a product group, cost object, or project.

The friend of the boss company VIP Optik messes up the entire production. The orders must be brought forward, the orders are processed in overtime and change requests to the models bring enormous challenges. More turnover, but and less contribution margin!

comparison plan- actual order

order no. 000010 prod. 111.010 classic glasses
responsibility Fritz Fleißig
period from 1801 to 1802

	DG 30	OT PA	OCL	OCAT PROD	BU 03	variance 22,3%
Plan			actual			variance
24 000,0			29 360,0			5 360,0

The deviation of the quantities is very positive at 22.3%

period 1802

Plan	actual	var.	description	cumulative Plan	in % OP	actual	in % OP	variance	
70.425,0	55.139,9	-21,7%	operation performance	140.850,0		156.865,9		16.015,9	11,4%
35.259,5	49.516,0	26,1%	use of goods	78.719,1	55,8%	99.232,0	63,2%	20.512,9	26,1%
116,7	143,0	22,6%	external capacity	233,0	0,2%	286,0	0,2%	52,7	22,6%
30.946,8	5.380,9	-82,6%	gross profit	61.897,6	43,9%	57.347,9	36,6%	-4.549,7	-7,4%
23.284,1	27.388,6	17,6%	activity costs	46.568,1	33,1%	66.411,7	42,3%	19.843,5	42,6%
		100,0%	other costs						
7.664,7	-22.007,7	-387,1%	Contribution margin II	15.329,5	10,9%	-9.063,8	-5,8%	-24.393,2	-159,1%
7.212,2	9.752,9	25,2%	fixed costs	14.424,4	10,2%	22.994,6	14,7%	8.570,3	59,4%
452,6	-31.760,6	-7.118,0%	result of performance	905,1	0,6%	-32.058,4	20,4%	-32.963,5	-3.641,9%

Plan	actual	var.	CTY	description	voucher no.	date	QU	Plan	actual	variance	%
65,4	65,4		91201	AU Bookkeeping				130,8	140,8	10,0	7,7%
64,8	103,7	60,0%	93001	AU purchasing				129,6	311,0	181,4	140,0%
			1801		180131	BEST					
			1802		180228	BEST					
				sums				12,00			

	quantity	price	total
	8,00	25,913	207,30
	4,00	25,913	103,65
	12,00		310,95

per	VT	W	source	CTY	text	CTV	var.	actual	variance	%
1801	B	1	KST3001	93001	No. of purchases		20,0%	480,0	639,9	80,0%
1802	B	1	KST3001	93001	No. of purchases		140,0%	3.099,8	6.716,3	260,0%
							100,0%	272,0	272,0	100,0%
					AU raw material storage		23,8%	2.174,1	836,9	23,8%
					AU production line		-36,0%	1.651,9	-619,5	-12,0%
					AU work preparation		23,8%	5.665,5	2.180,8	23,8%
					AU metalworking					
					AU plastic injection molding					
					AU spraying plastic splashes					

The deviation in the use of goods and the processes must be analyzed and consequences drawn from it...! The production management was only able to fulfill customer requirements with overtime. See the variances in the processes of cost center 400 Production Management.

Figure 10 Plan / Actual Article Glasses Classic

89

Step 6. Plausibility
Coordination & reasonability of planning

In this phase, we speak of the kneading of planning.
We try everything! Are all performances actually
charged? Has everyone checked their revenues,
costs, processes, and performance?
Has the entire performance volume potential been
charged?

How do you test whether it is even possible to
achieve the planned sales figures with your
company image, sales, products, or the services of
your company?

Customers value analysis

We use the customer value analysis of Schauenburg for this verification. Schauenburg has developed a system for competition comparison, he set up a criteria structure according to a scheme and then evaluates the used criteria.

The customer value arises from the market position and the product value. This, in turn, consists of the technical, commercial, and operational value, etc.

Please, take a look at the figure below, where a review of a criteria structure of a Businessplan Indicator is shown.

PU = Product Utility
MP = Market Position
M + A = Merger + Acquisitions

Figure 11 Costumer value analysis Schauenburg

The value which the customers actually take advantage of, become the **key to the market success**.

Your advantages

- You should regulate and systematize the **customer information** (e.g. from competition studies, customer surveys or market observations)
- You should determine the **customer expectations** and make them transparent
- You should develop a better **customer understanding**
- You should make more accurate **customer orientation**

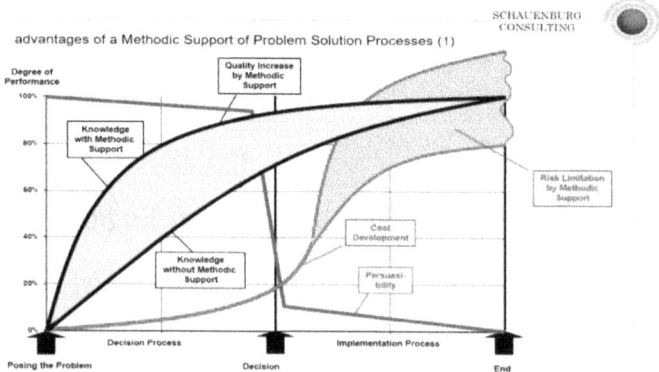

Figure 12 Decision maker Source Schauenburg

All results (quantity x price tag) are split to cost centers or on cost objects as performance processes. See also Illustration 14 "Performance totals". The check shows: everything is charged.

						performance totals
1	120	1	No. of bookings	BOOK	30 000.0	30 000.0	30 000.0
1	120	2	LE Capture bookings	No	6 000.0	6 000.0	6 000.0
1	120	3	LE Debit customer base	No	2 000.0	2 000.0	2 000.0
1	120	4	LE Debit credit check	No	250.0	250.0	250.0
1	120	5	LE Debit dunning	No	1 200.0	1 200.0	1 200.0
1	120	6	LE Edit debit outages	No	20.0	20.0	20.0
1	120	7	LE Debit letters write	Mail	210.0	210.0	210.0
1	120	9	LE Debit Team Leading	Hour	10.0	10.0	10.0

Figure 14 Performance Management

- Does the employee know the goals of the contribution margins?
- Are the capacities of the strategic projects planned?
- Where is the customer in relation to the margins?

In this phase the inefficiencies that have been dragged along for years come to light! The analytical planning means some effort, but this is worthwhile not only now and also in the future.

Step 7. Account of actual cost
Actual activity recording

Our claim to the account of actual cost is quality and speed. The account of actual cost and, importantly, the performance recording, is already considered in the planning. Planning without actual data is pointless!

The costs and revenues should not cause any problems. The import is regulated and the data records are stored accordingly from the financial accounting. A concept of an account assignment is created and the data is checked for plausibility during the import.

Corresponding error messages are immediately displayed in a separate column. In order to get a quick grip on the errors, there is a possibility to make relevant transfers, but it is also possible to allocate cost centers, cost types or cost objects. Of course, the assignment should also be changed by the sender.

data Source

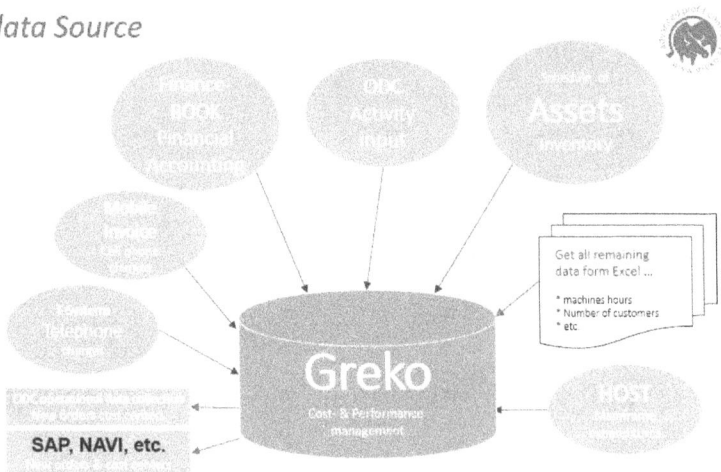

Figure 15 data source

It needs to be clearly stated that "tally charts" are not a suitable performance recording tool.

Therefore, from the beginning, it is advisable to introduce a recording tool.

This database must be able to record the results as a minimum requirement, at least in Excel, and be able to transfer the data automatically. As a result, we always find a way which everyone involved can live with!

Your advantages

- Detect incorrect account assignments during import

- Plausibility check program controlled at the push of a button in all data areas

- Simple, uncomplicated re-accountability options

- Access and evaluation options for those responsible for self-regulation

- Basis for building a scorecard

Step 8. Analyzes & Evaluations
Detection – improvement - avoidance

Who has sown, can now begin the harvest!

Next to the surprises of the inefficiencies from the planning - see metaphor "dripping faucet" – now comes to the most beautiful part. Each responsible person evaluates their data according to the principle of

"*autonomous self-management*".

The target / actual data comparison, in contrast to the plan / actual data comparison, shows the true, economic statement of a cost center. This way, the excuses of employees will be severely limited in the future.

The stepwise contribution accounting shows the performance quantity allocation of the sender (cost centers / reference quantities) to the cost object.

This way the person in charge can see very clearly who has exceeded their performance according to the planning.

The improvements will be closely followed in the next months.

Thus, all employees recognize how the costs are related to the performance volume.

This transparency helps with all improvements to initiate the correct improvement measures.

Your advantages

- Visualization of the performance – scorecard
- Improvements become measurable
- Tops / flops price tag / cost objects / customers
- Deviations in the cost centers due to the **"real"** target / actual comparisons
- Performance cost transparency
- Customer CM account

Reading list

Time-Driven Activity-Based Costing:
Robert Steven Kaplan

Beyond Budgeting
Niels Pfläging

Process Compliant Resource Consumption
Accounting Heinrich Müller

Flexible Budget Accounting and Contribution
Accounting Wolfgang Kilger

Coaching and Leading with System
Dieter Bischop

Customer Value Analysis
Jochen Schauenburg

Leading with Flexible Goals
Niels Pfläging

On our behalf
advanced profit control

The apc is an independent business consulting company that was established as a unyielding network of self-employed experts.

My company is called advanced profit control. First of all, I would like to clarify that this does not mean "cost cutting". My goal is to uncover inefficiencies in order to increase capacity and pinpoint the time for innovation.

In doing the following, we want to ensure that transparency is created, so that team leaders and owners, as well as the management, and the employees themselves, can see how diligent the employees are within the company.

apc offers consulting services for corporate governance & management with the main focuses:

Comprehensive corporate management

- Strategic & operational business planning
- Implementation support

Cost and performance management

- Product / article process calculation
- Target costing
- Stepwise contribution accounting
- Sales controlling
- Division accounting and much more

Team leader information

- Transparency of performance and costs
- Structure of the company-individual scorecard

The key difference to other "advisors" is that we, in addition to the analytical advice, also engage in active implementation and install a methodology that allows us to measure, manage, and control performance in a long-term perspective.

By combining team leadership skills and business process modeling with a software tool, apc differs substantially from our valued competitors.

In the following, apc develops and distributes database-based software for process compliant Resource Consumption Accounting as a decision-making tool for executives.

In this context, apc and its cooperation partners provide consulting services and

provide methodological know-how for the implementation, integration, and deployment optimization of this software among their customers.

apc cooperates with network partners in
Austria, Hungary, Germany and Switzerland.
Our customers come from all over the world.

Abbreviations

ORT	Order type
VAR	Variance
ORGR	Order group
ORCAT	Order category
ORD	Order
OASGR	OAS group
OASGO	OAS goals
BGGR	Budget group
BGPOS	Budget position
CMGR	CM group
CMGO	CM goals
FIX	Fix costs
FCR	Fix cost rate
BU	Business unit
MC	Marginal cost
MCR	Marginal cost rate
PRC	Payroll costs
ICA	Internal cost allocation
CT	Cost type
CC	Cost center
CIP	Continuous Improvement Process
IWC	Incidental wage costs
MSC	management success calculation
PU	Price unit
PAC	plan / actual comparison
SFC	Staff costs
PROP	Proportional costs
PT	Process time
SORD	Standard order
TAC	Target / actual comparison
CCC	Charging calculated costs

Index

Illustrations

Notice for doni (Day of new ideas)

Notice for doni (Day of new ideas)

Notice for doni (Day of new ideas)

Notice for doni (Day of new ideas)

Notice for doni (Day of new ideas)

Notice for doni (Day of new ideas)

Notice for doni (Day of new ideas)

Notice for doni (Day of new ideas)

Notice for doni (Day of new ideas)

Notice for doni (Day of new ideas)

Notice for doni (Day of new ideas)

Notice for doni (Day of new ideas)

Notice for doni (Day of new ideas)

Notice for doni (Day of new ideas)

www.ingramcontent.com/pod-product-compliance
Lightning Source LLC
Chambersburg PA
CBHW061258220326
41599CB00028B/5694